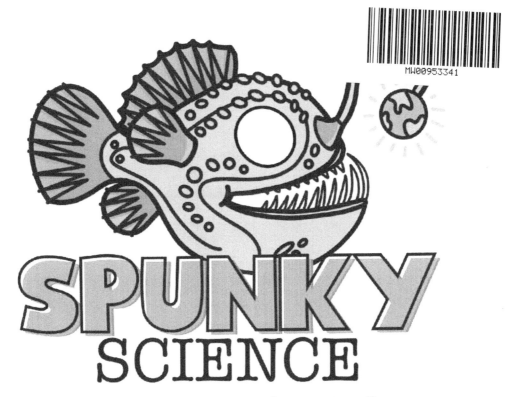

SPUNKY SCIENCE

Copyright © 2022 Spunky Science

MW00953341

TABLE OF CONTENTS

SPUNKY SCIENCE

MATTER & ITS INTERACTIONS

Substances are made of different kinds of atoms, which combine with one another in various ways. Atoms form molecules that range in size from 2-2,000 atoms.

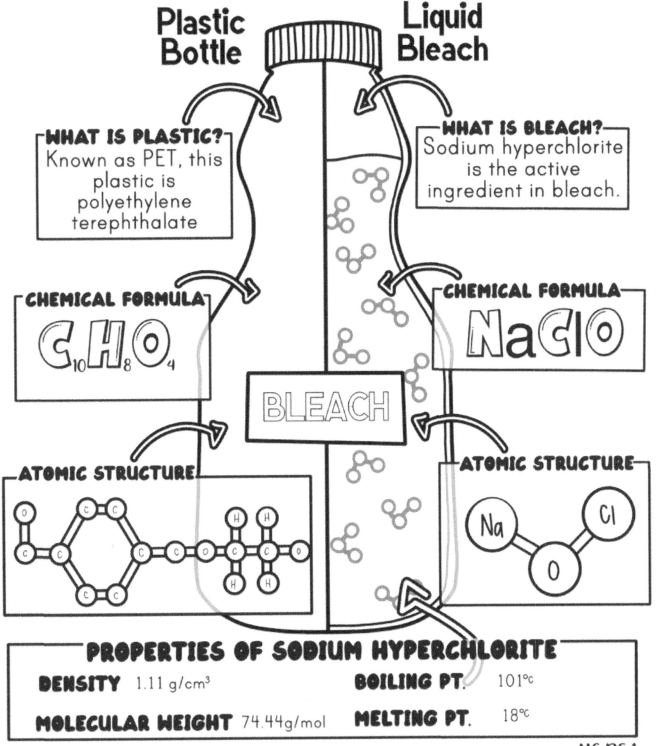

Plastic Bottle

Liquid Bleach

WHAT IS PLASTIC?
Known as PET, this plastic is polyethylene terephthalate

WHAT IS BLEACH?
Sodium hyperchlorite is the active ingredient in bleach.

CHEMICAL FORMULA
$C_{10}H_8O_4$

CHEMICAL FORMULA
$NaClO$

BLEACH

ATOMIC STRUCTURE

ATOMIC STRUCTURE

PROPERTIES OF SODIUM HYPERCHLORITE

DENSITY 1.11 g/cm³

BOILING PT. 101°c

MOLECULAR WEIGHT 74.44g/mol

MELTING PT. 18°c

PHYSICAL PROPERTIES

Physical properties can be observed or measured without changing the composition of matter.

DENSITY

Ethyl Alcohol
Olive Oil
Water
Liquid Soap
Honey

MELTING POINT

BOILING POINT

SOLUBILITY

MASS

ODOR

COLOR

Cute Potato

LENGTH

Spunky Science ™

CHEMICAL PROPERTIES

Each pure substance has characteristic physical and chemical properties (for any bulk quantity under given conditions) that could be used to identify it.

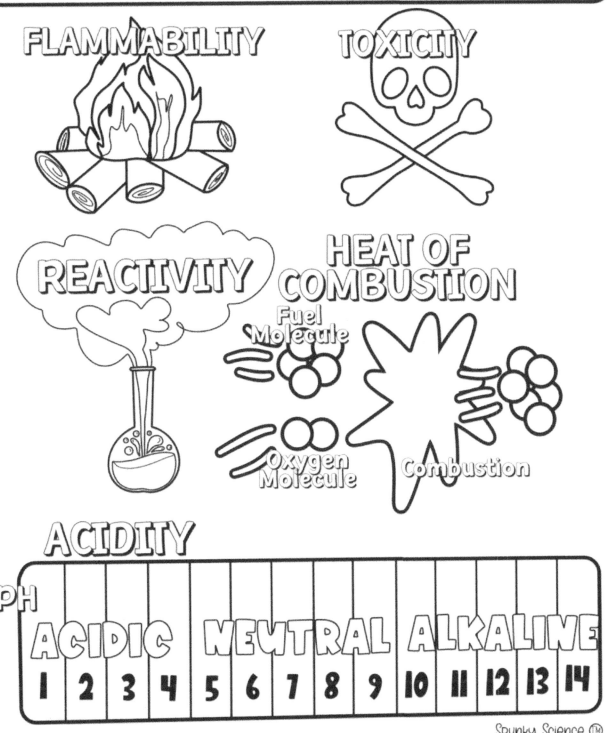

FLAMMABILITY

TOXICITY

REACTIVITY

HEAT OF COMBUSTION

Fuel Molecule

Oxygen Molecule

Combustion

ACIDITY

PH	ACIDIC				NEUTRAL					ALKALINE				
	1	2	3	4	5	6	7	8	9	10	11	12	13	14

GAS

Gases and liquids are made of molecules or inert atoms that are moving about relative to each other.

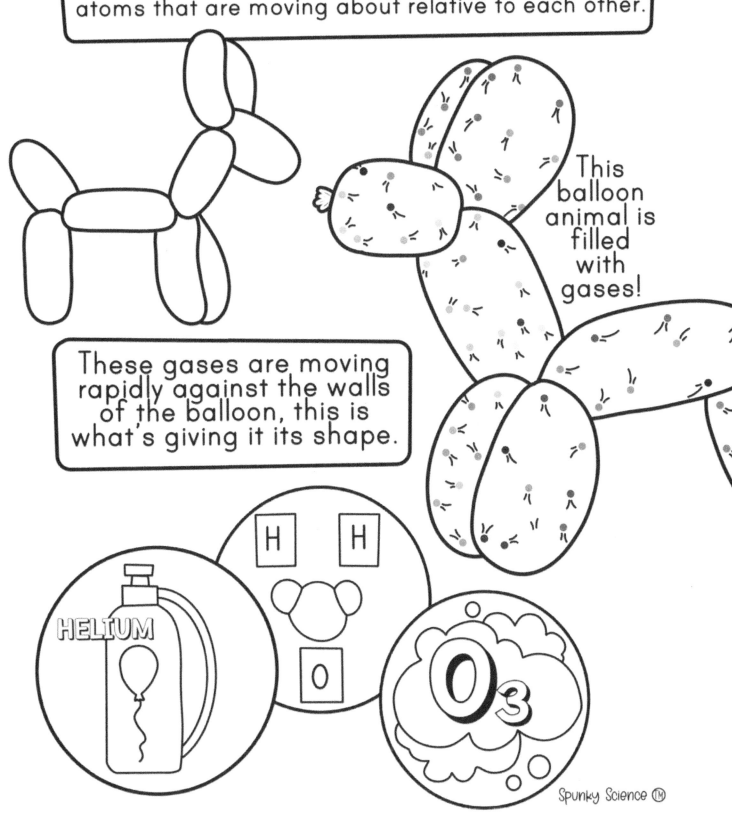

This balloon animal is filled with gases!

These gases are moving rapidly against the walls of the balloon, this is what's giving it its shape.

HELIUM

H H

O

O₃

Spunky Science ™

LIQUIDS

In a liquid, the molecules are constantly in contact with others; in a gas, they are widely spaced, except when they happen to collide.

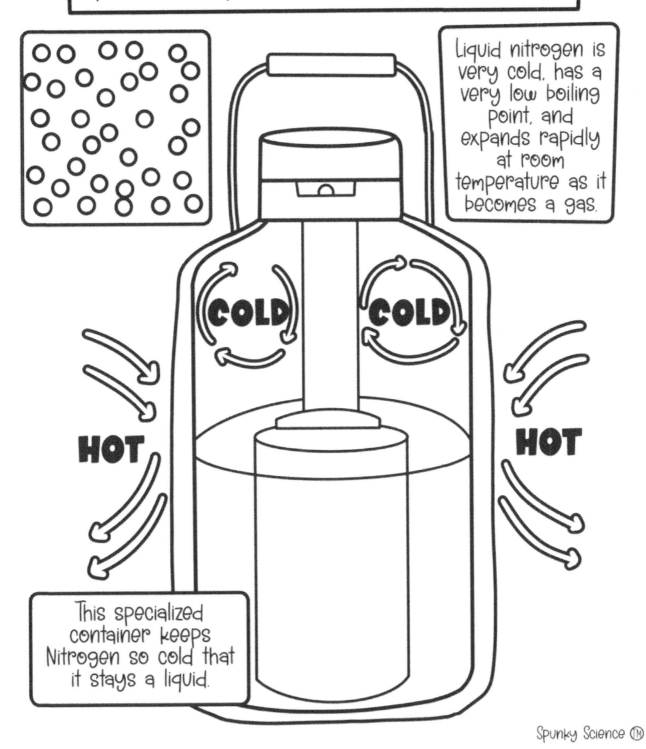

Liquid nitrogen is very cold, has a very low boiling point, and expands rapidly at room temperature as it becomes a gas.

COLD COLD

HOT HOT

This specialized container keeps Nitrogen so cold that it stays a liquid.

Spunky Science ™

SOLIDS

Solids may be formed from molecules, or they may be extended structures with repeating subunits.

In a solid, Atoms are closely spaced and may vibrate in position, but do not change relative locations.

SOLID

SOLID

SOLID CRYSTAL

Spunky Science ™

HEAT & PRESSURE

The changes of state that occur with variations and temperature or pressure can be described and predicted using these models of matter.

PRESSURE COOKER

Valve

A sealed chamber that traps the steam generated as its contents are heated.

Rubber sealing ring

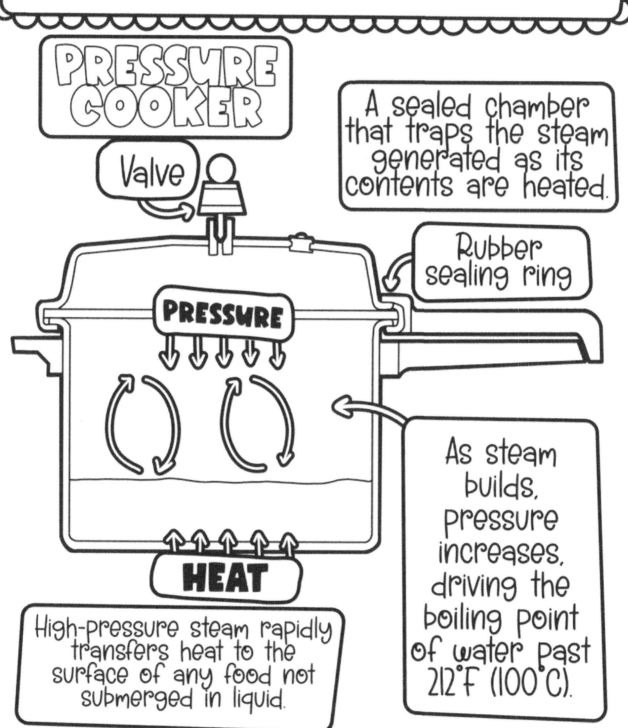

PRESSURE

HEAT

High-pressure steam rapidly transfers heat to the surface of any food not submerged in liquid.

As steam builds, pressure increases, driving the boiling point of water past 212°F (100°C).

Spunky Science ™

CHEMICAL REACTIONS

Substances react chemically in characteristic ways. In a chemical process, the atoms that make up the original substances are regrouped into different molecules, and these new substances have different properties from those of the reactants.

Burning Sugar

$$6O_2 + C_6H_{12}O_6$$
$$6H_2O + 6CO_2$$

Burning Steel Wool

$$FE + O2$$
$$FE2O3$$

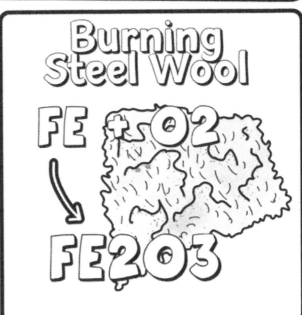

Fat Reacting with Sodium Hydroxide

SOAPONIFICATION

Zinc + Hydrogen Chloride

$$Zn + HCl$$

YIELDS

$$ZnCl_2 + H_2$$

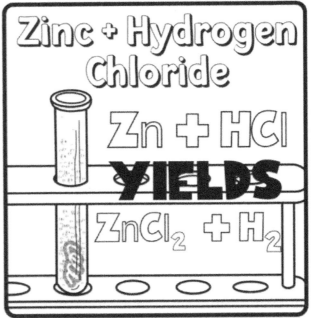

CONSERVATION OF MASS

The total number of each type of atom is conserved, and thus the mass does not change.

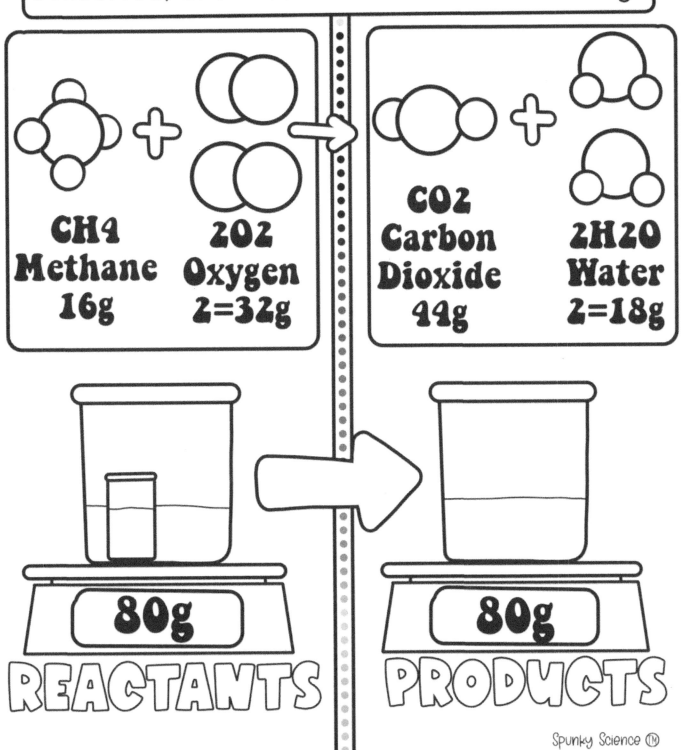

CH4
Methane
16g

2O2
Oxygen
2=32g

CO2
Carbon
Dioxide
44g

2H2O
Water
2=18g

80g

80g

REACTANTS

PRODUCTS

Spunky Science ™

ENERGY IN REACTIONS

Some chemical reactions release energy, while others store energy.

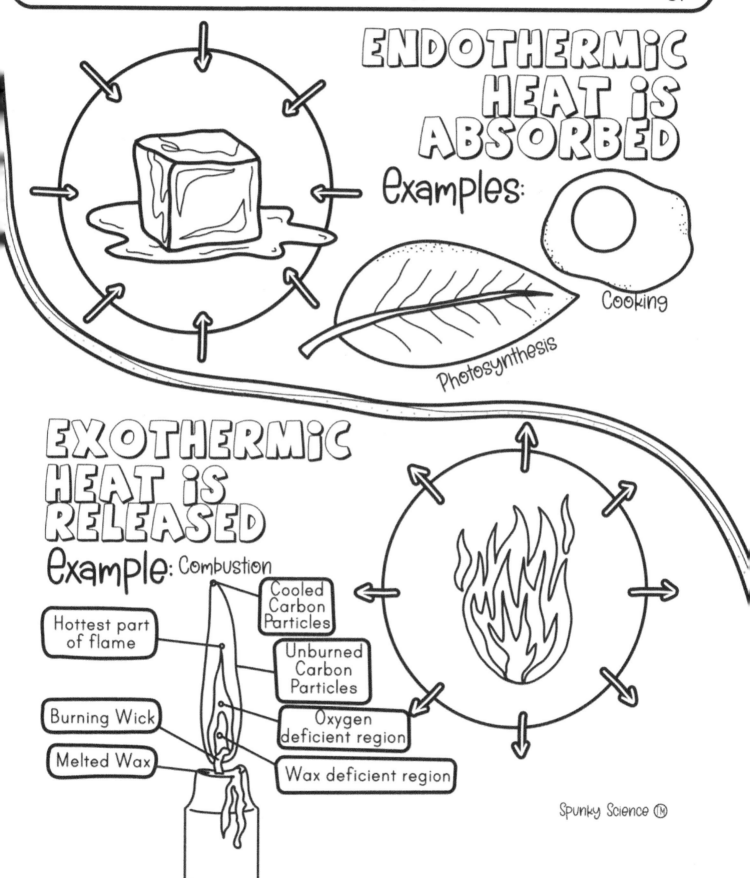

ENDOTHERMIC HEAT IS ABSORBED

Examples:

Photosynthesis

Cooking

EXOTHERMIC HEAT IS RELEASED

Example: Combustion

Hottest part of flame

Burning Wick

Melted Wax

Cooled Carbon Particles

Unburned Carbon Particles

Oxygen deficient region

Wax deficient region

Spunky Science ™

THERMAL TRANSFER

In science, heat refers to the energy transfer due to the temperature difference between two objects.

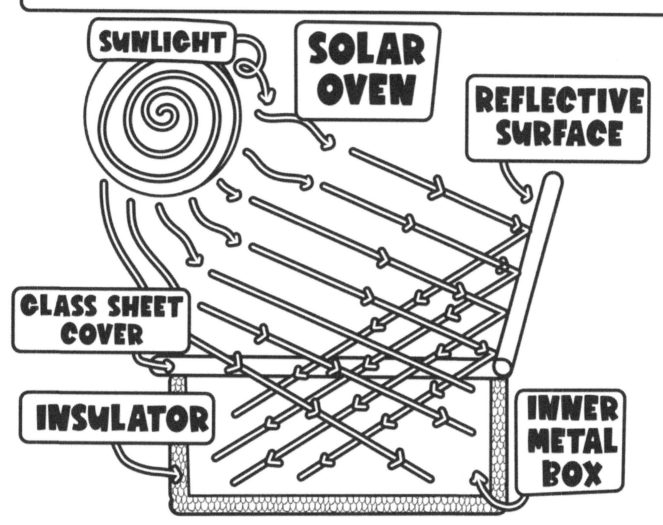

SUNLIGHT

SOLAR OVEN

REFLECTIVE SURFACE

GLASS SHEET COVER

INSULATOR

INNER METAL BOX

HOW A SOLAR OVEN WORKS

1. Sunlight enters the oven.
2. The dark interior, pots and lids absorb light, transforming the sun's energy into heat.
3. Heat is trapped inside-an environmentally beneficial use of the greenhouse effect.

POTENTIAL AND KINETIC ENERGY

INTERNAL ENERGY=KINETIC ENERGY • POTENTIAL ENERGY

The temperature of a system is proportional to the average internal kinetic energy and the potential energy per atom or molecule.

$$U = E_K + E_P$$

Internal Energy-E
The sum of all the kinetic & potential energies of all the atom and molecules in a sample.

LAW OF CONSERVATION OF ENERGY: The total energy of universe is constant

KINETIC & TEMPERATURE

Measure the degree of hotness and coldness of a system

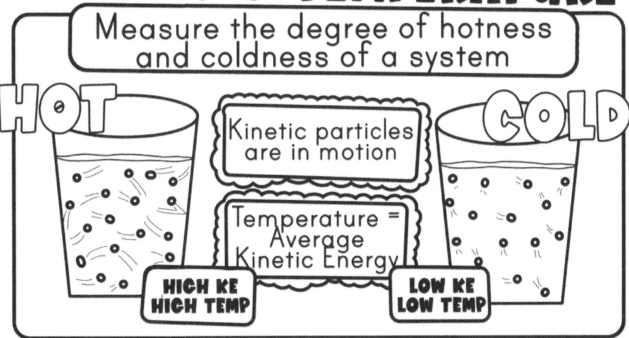

HOT

COLD

Kinetic particles are in motion

Temperature = Average Kinetic Energy

HIGH KE HIGH TEMP

LOW KE LOW TEMP

MATTER & ITS INTERACTIONS

```
C E O J D E Y F L P T W E R U S S E R P
O S D I U Q I L J A S R B O V I E P I T
N E K T C I C A U T C I M R E H T O X E
S N W R I R A F C O I N Y Q J G Q A J O
E D A A R O Y K W M K C Q E L S E D G P
R O G N M J L S A I F X T G C E H N D N
V T P S O O V H T C H E M I C A L L A O
E H M F A L I J A E O I B K V I G V I I
D E B E W D G E L E L M Z S P L U B E T
K R C R A J X H C R I S A J F T R E N I
P M R R Z P W K P U R E C V A H S P O S
G I S E H Y H D A T L K J X N S A H P O
A C K D O R G A S E S E P S S E C O R P
A L P S E R U T C U R T S P O K M V E M
Z I A G K L N O K O O B V V V L O S W O
C D W P F B B M R E A C T I O N S A S C
M S E I A T X S L A N O I T R O P O R P
```

Atomic	Pure	Inert	Endothermic
Composition	Chemical	Pressure	Exothermic
Molecules	Liquids	Reactions	Crystals
Structures	Gases	Process	Transferred
Atoms		Conserved	Proportional

MOTION & STABILITY: FORCES & INTERACTIONS

NEWTON'S THIRD LAW

For every action there is an equal and opposite reaction.

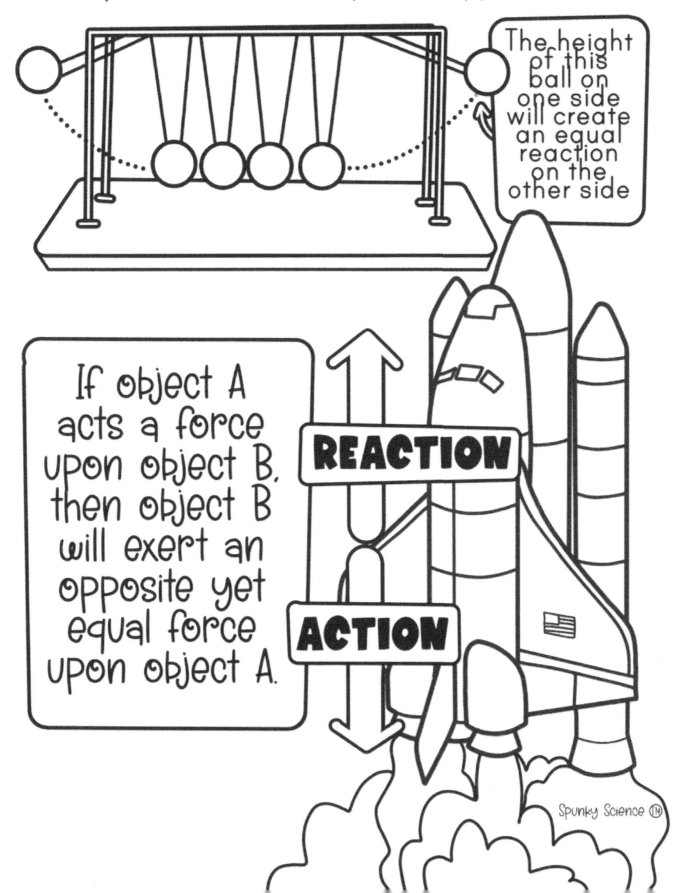

The height of this ball on one side will create an equal reaction on the other side

If object A acts a force upon object B, then object B will exert an opposite yet equal force upon object A.

REACTION

ACTION

Spunky Science ™

BALANCED & UNBALANCED FORCES

The motion of an object is determined by the sum of the forces acting onto it.

If the total force on the object is not zero, it's motion will change.

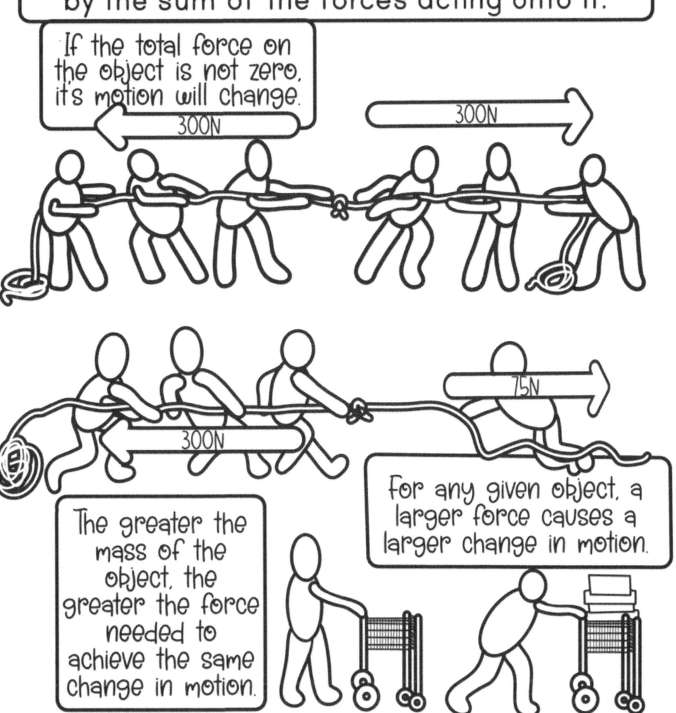

The greater the mass of the object, the greater the force needed to achieve the same change in motion.

For any given object, a larger force causes a larger change in motion.

FORCE DIAGRAMS

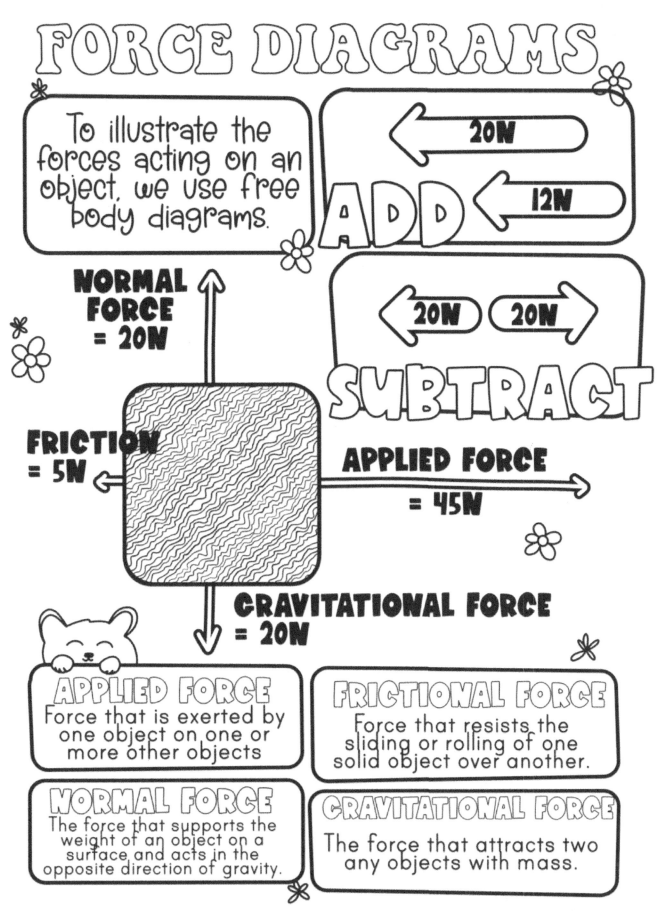

To illustrate the forces acting on an object, we use free body diagrams.

ADD
20N
12N

SUBTRACT
20N 20N

NORMAL FORCE = 20N

FRICTION = 5N

APPLIED FORCE = 45N

GRAVITATIONAL FORCE = 20N

APPLIED FORCE
Force that is exerted by one object on one or more other objects

FRICTIONAL FORCE
Force that resists the sliding or rolling of one solid object over another.

NORMAL FORCE
The force that supports the weight of an object on a surface and acts in the opposite direction of gravity.

GRAVITATIONAL FORCE
The force that attracts two any objects with mass.

Spunky Science ™

ELECTROMAGNETIC FORCES

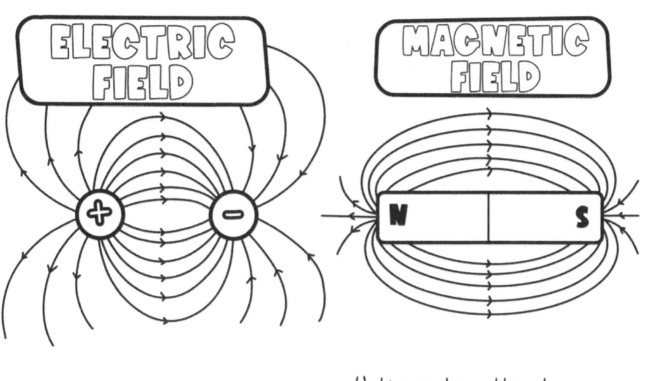

ELECTRIC FIELD

MAGNETIC FIELD

Electric and magnetic can be attractive or repulsive.

Unlike poles attract

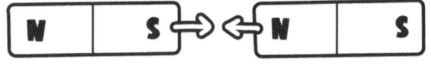

| N | S | ⇒ ⇐ | N | S |

| S | N | ⇒ ⇐ | S | N |

Like poles repel

| S | N | ⇐ ⇒ | N | S |

| N | S | ⇐ ⇒ | S | N |

Their sizes depend on the magnitude of the charges, currents, or magnetic strength involved and on the distances between the interacting objects.

GRAVITATIONAL FORCES

The forces of attraction between any two bodies in the Universe.

The earths gravitational pull on a body lying near the surface of Earth.

GRAVITY

There's a gravitational force between any two masses. The larger the object, the greater the gravitational pull.

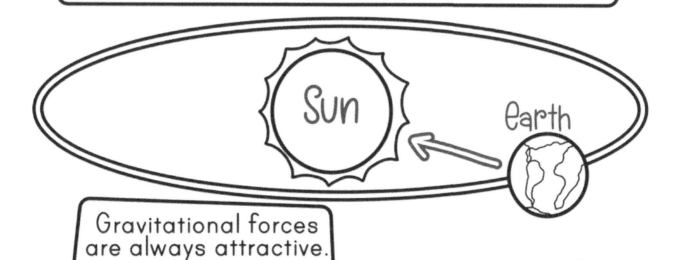

Sun

earth

Gravitational forces are always attractive.

MOTION & STABILITY

```
P M A G N E T I C L C D C L S T R E X E
A A L S O A O K T R V F G K V Y O I F Q
T G K A D I S T A N C E R H R O I S K U
T N E L E C T R O M A G N E T I C N S A
R I H J M P C S V X C H A R G E S O U L
A T O U N W H D B C U I S O O G E T Q D
C U P I R Z G O N E R S R T B H I W S K
T D H O F H D P T R R D E T R R O E E S
I E B M O T I O N I E O P N C E C N N O
V P C H R I L S H O N E U V D E N I I A
E Z S F C P H I E D T R L R E C L G Q L
M S A D E O W T I S I B S D W N D E T X
N N E S S N Q I O A H S I I Q M G B N H
L K O S H V Z O P N F A V O A I J E R E
K E L P S S D N N R S P E P D Y O Q E R
N R A I I A N E B E A C S T C E J B O I
T D W V O H M L A N O I T A T I V A R G
```

Forces   Newton   Attractive   Distance

Motion   Law   Repulsive   Gravitational

Objects   Position   Magnitude   Electromagnetic

Equal   Electric   Charges   Strength

Exerts   Magnetic   Current   Masses

ENERGY

KINETIC ENERGY

Kinetic energy is directly proportional to the mass of the object and to the square of its velocity.

$$K.E. = 1/2 \, MV^2$$

Kinetic energy   Mass   Velocity

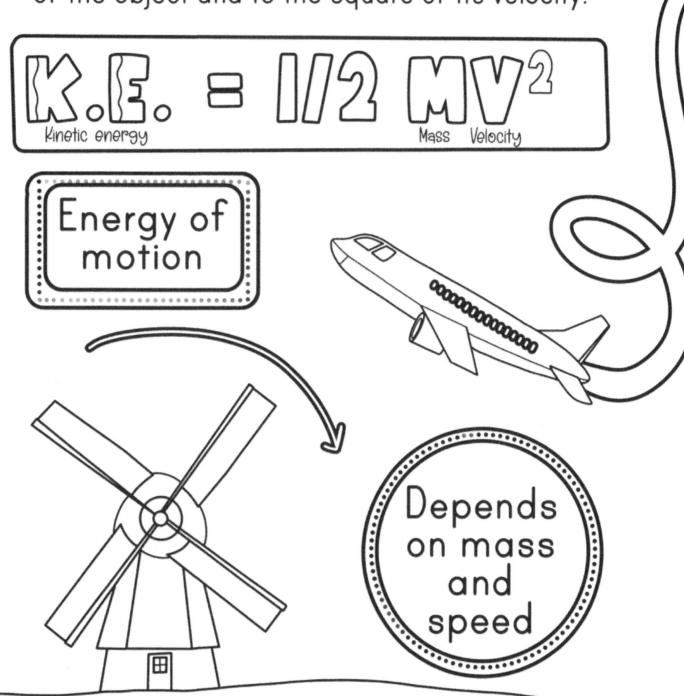

Energy of motion

Depends on mass and speed

POTENTIAL ENERGY

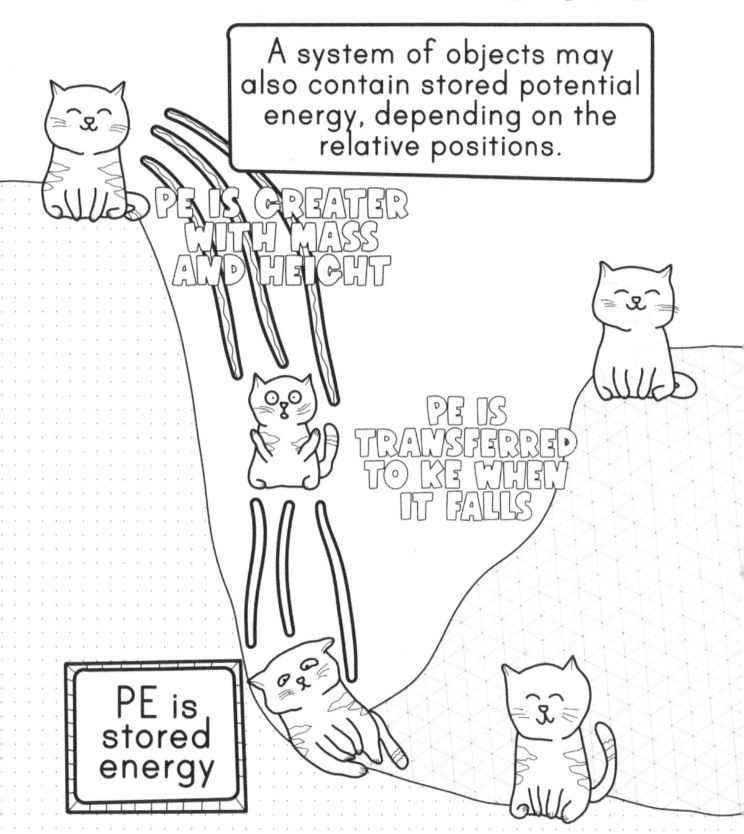

A system of objects may also contain stored potential energy, depending on the relative positions.

PE IS GREATER WITH MASS AND HEIGHT

PE IS TRANSFERRED TO KE WHEN IT FALLS

PE is stored energy

Spunky Science ™

TEMPERATURE & ENERGY

Temperature is a measure of the average kinetic energy of particles of matter.

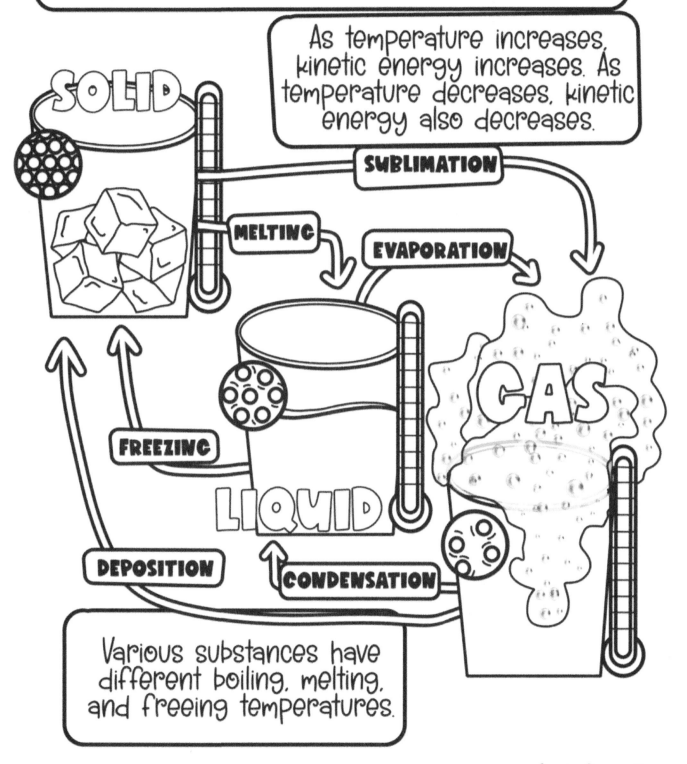

As temperature increases, kinetic energy increases. As temperature decreases, kinetic energy also decreases.

SOLID

SUBLIMATION

MELTING

EVAPORATION

GAS

FREEZING

LIQUID

DEPOSITION

CONDENSATION

Various substances have different boiling, melting, and freeing temperatures.

PE/KE TRANSFER

When the motion energy of an object changes, there is inevitably some other changes in energy at the same time.

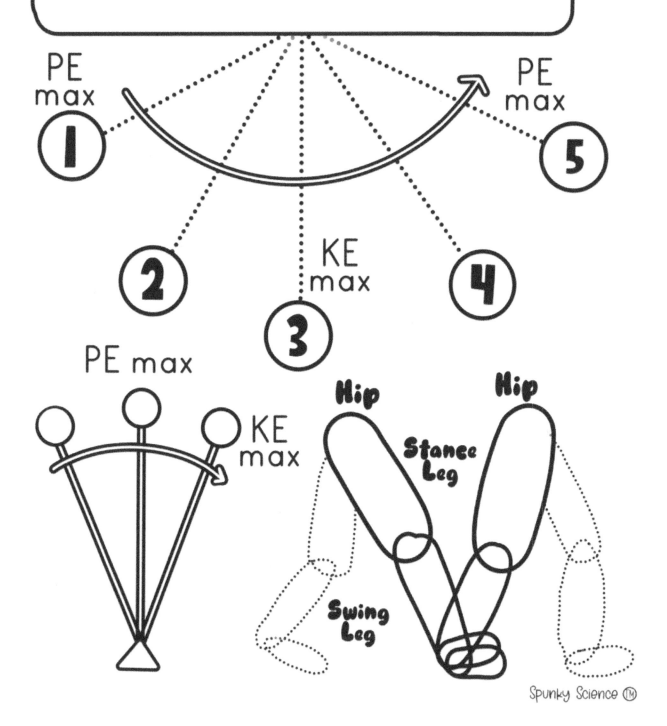

PE max — ①

PE max — ②

KE max — ③

④

PE max — ⑤

PE max

KE max

Hip

Stance Leg

Hip

Swing Leg

Spunky Science ™

CHANGING
STATES OF MATTER

ADDING HEAT

REMOVING HEAT

SOLID

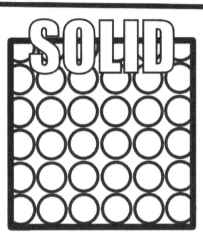

Tightly packed molecules vibrate

LIQUID

Loosely packed molecules

Takes the shape of the container

GAS

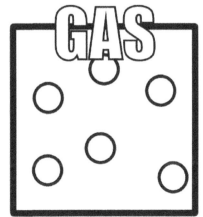

Fills space

moves freely

Spunky Science ™

ENERGY TRANSFER

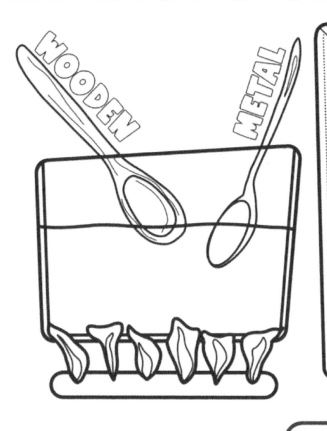

WOODEN

METAL

The amount of energy transfer needed to change the temperature of a matter sample by given amount depends on the nature of the matter, the size of the sample, and the environment.

The beaker with more water will take longer to heat up.

Spunky Science ™

THERMAL ENERGY TRANSFER

Energy is spontaneously transferred out of hotter, regions or objects and into colder ones.

Thermal energy always moves from warmer to cooler objects

BUBBLE WATER

Heat moves from the cans and into the ice until they are the same temperature.

Spunky Science ™

INTERACTING FORCES

When two objects interact, each one exert to force on the other that can cause energy to be transferred to or from the object.

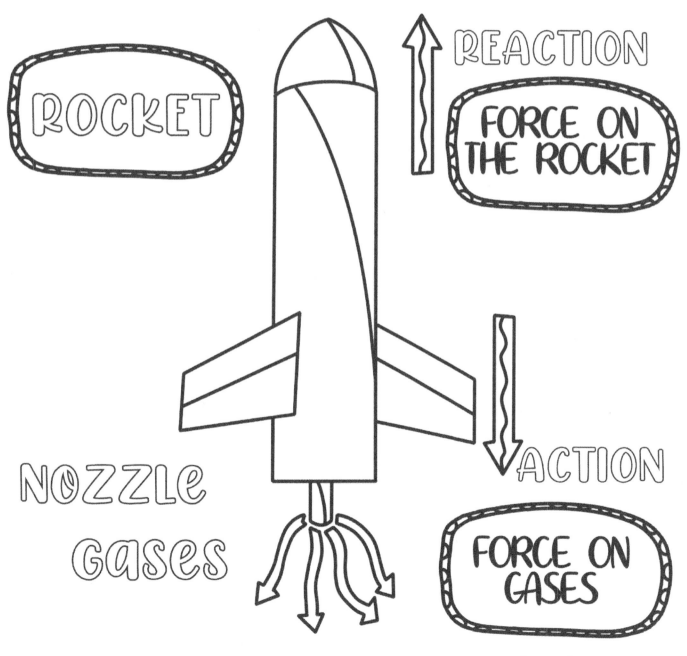

ROCKET

REACTION
FORCE ON THE ROCKET

ACTION
FORCE ON GASES

NOZZLE gases

ENERGY

```
P I V E N V I R O N M E N T L T G O T A
A S A V S I S J H R O G O L P A M I S W
R Z X I W L F A O B J E C T S S N U T E
T A E T D E X Z T W R O C O F F C H O H
I W F A H D M O T I O N U I B H S B R J
C F B L U G T X E S V A R A T H D G E H
L B J E L T I V R L D S E S Z E E V D F
E Y P R O P O R T I O N A L X G N D K D
S U L M R J L O G N I V O M C M U I L V
L O M A V E R A G E B R N Y B N Y N K F
W L Y P K J F P V L R T M R G F E Y B O
X M D E E P S S Z Q D H R E U R R F G R
Z L X F G K A S N Z W C I T E N E K D C
A M A T T E R T A A A Q O A W F F N S E
S P K J A G B L Q M R W W S S S U O E S
F F L Q Q D V M T O I T E O T D P Y V G
C O L D E R Q T M M N O I T I S O P U F
```

Motion	Speed	Particles	Colder
Energy	Stored	Transfer	Forces
Proportional	Relative	Matter	Objects
Mass	Position	Environment	Moving
Average	Kinetic	Hotter	

WAVES AND THEIR APPLICATIONS IN TECHNOLOGIES FOR INFORMATION TRASNFER

WAVES

A simple wave has a repeating pattern with a specific wavelength, frequency, and amplitude.

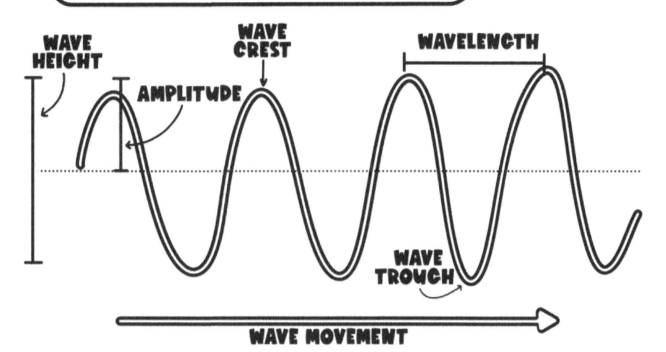

WAVE HEIGHT

AMPLITUDE

WAVE CREST

WAVELENGTH

WAVE TROUGH

WAVE MOVEMENT

TYPES OF ELECTROMAGENTIC RADIATION

RADIO
Used to broadcast radio and television

MICROWAVES
Used in cooking, radar, telephone and other signals

INFRARED
Transmits heat from sun, fires, and radiators

VISIBLE LIGHT
Makes things able to be seen

ULTRAVIOLET
Absorbed by the skin and used in fluorescent tubes

X-RAYS
Used to view inside of bodies and objects

GAMMA RAYS
Used in medicine for killing cancer cells

Spunky Science ™

SOUND WAVE

A soundwave needs a medium through which it is transmitted.

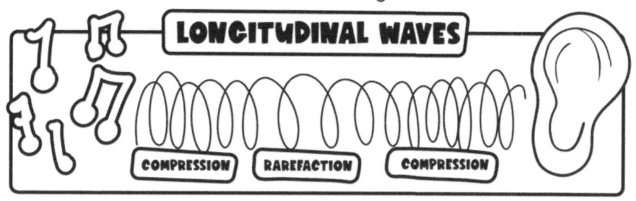

LONGITUDINAL WAVES

COMPRESSION RAREFACTION COMPRESSION

QUIETER

AMPLITUDE

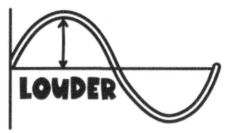

LOUDER

LOWER PITCH

HIGHER PITCH

NO MOTION	SLOWEST $\longrightarrow$		FASTEST
VACUUM	GAS	LIQUID	SOLID

ELECTROMAGNETIC RADIATION

When light shines in an object, it is reflected, absorbed, or transmitted through the object, depending on the objects material and the frequency of the light.

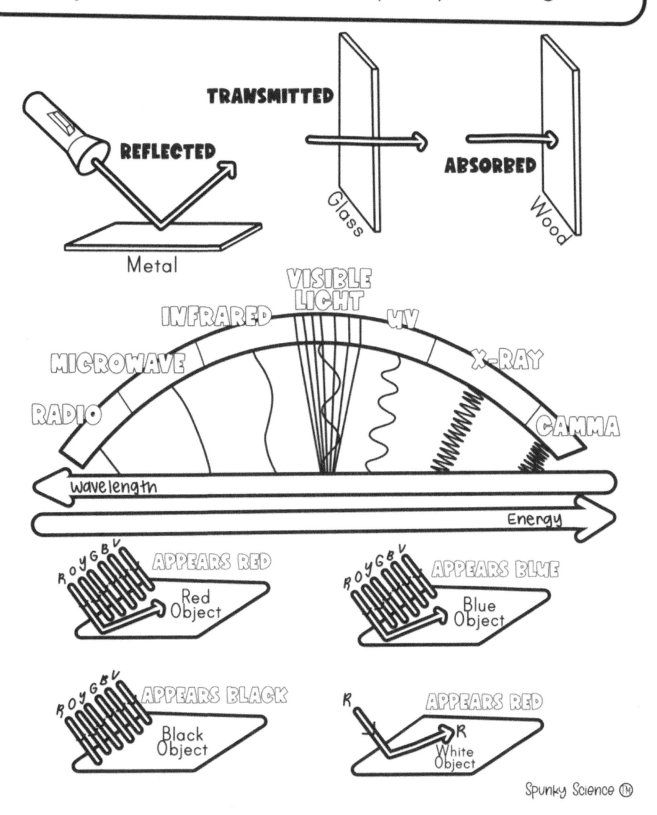

REFLECTED

TRANSMITTED

ABSORBED

Metal

Glass

Wood

VISIBLE LIGHT

INFRARED

MICROWAVE

UV

X-RAY

RADIO

GAMMA

wavelength

Energy

ROYGBV APPEARS RED
Red Object

ROYGBV APPEARS BLUE
Blue Object

ROYGBV APPEARS BLACK
Black Object

R APPEARS RED
White Object

Spunky Science ™

LIGHT PATH

The path that light travels can be traced as straight lines, except the surfaces between different transparent materials where the light path bends.

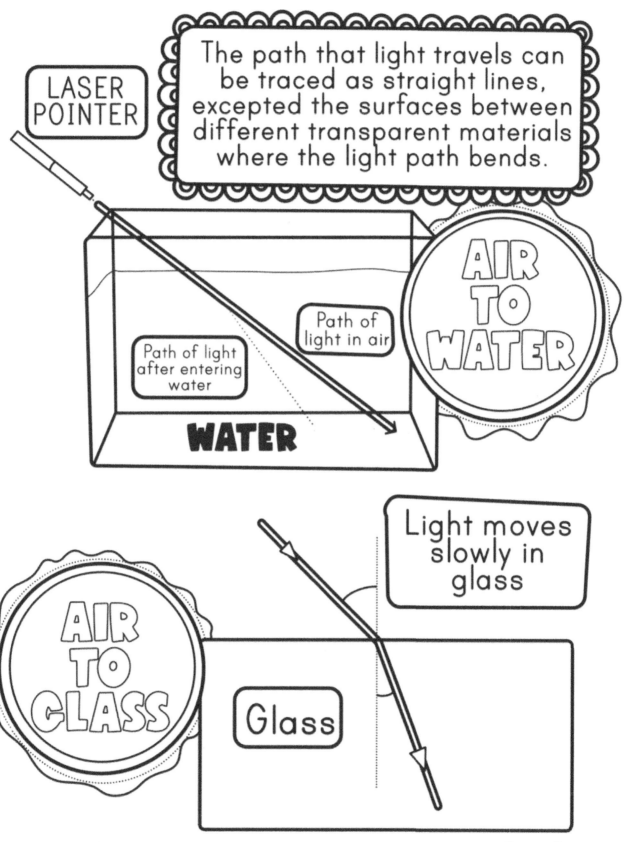

LASER POINTER

AIR TO WATER

Path of light in air

Path of light after entering water

WATER

AIR TO GLASS

Glass

Light moves slowly in glass

PRISMS

A wave model of light is useful for explaining brightness, color, and the frequency-dependent bending of light at a surface between media.

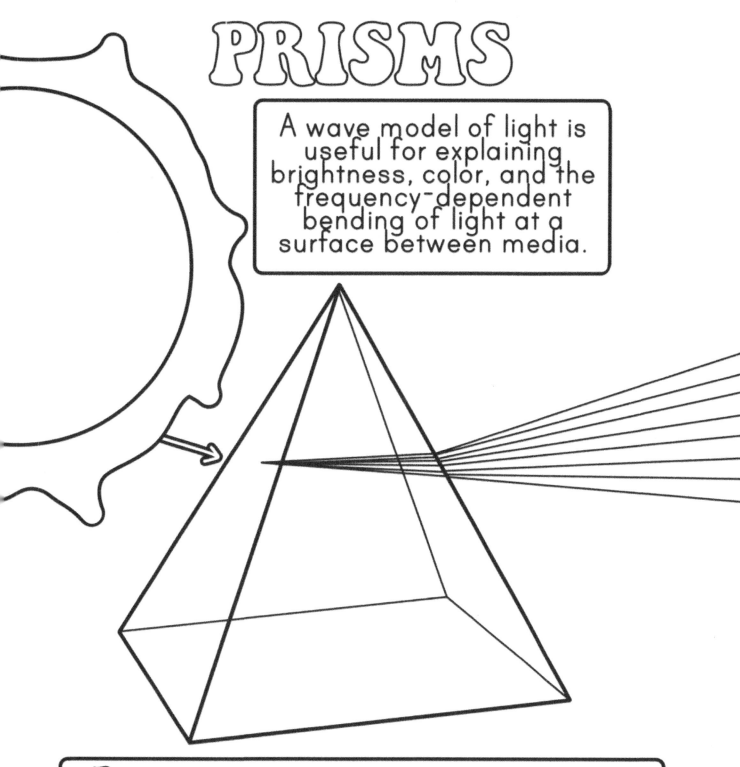

Triangular prism refracts the light source and splits it into different colors, allowing a full spectrum of rainbow colors to appear in your photography.

Spunky Science ™

INFORMATION TECHNOLOGIES AND INSTRUMENTATION

Digitized signals (sent as wave pulses) are a more reliable way to encoding transmit information than analog signals.

ANALOG SIGNAL

If signal is weak, picture is weak along with a lot of static

DIGITAL SIGNAL

As long as the TV is receiving a signal, the picture is perfect.

ANALOG SIGNAL

Both signals weaken with distance

DIGITAL SIGNAL

Spunky Science ™

WAVES

```
P W A V E L E N G T H G O R O C R S U A
L H I I J E H T W X R F P E S M E W T W
B K O O L V K H A C J A S S O S F G I M
E L T A L C P F V V O J V B D O L U M E
N P N M M E K D E B P O J E P A E O S D
D L O P G R F R S Y L K I H L N C P N I
S M I L D A B S O R B E D O S V T K A U
I V T I Z O S I J G S O U N D H E H R M
G D A T X P N O T J T E O F T G D E T O
N W M U V U O R U O I V I A Y I R D K E
A X R D K L I G H T I J T T O Q P Z L C
L F O E P S T Y C N E U Q E R F A C D A
O T F H P E A K W E B N I I C E S M Q F
K H N J C S I L A R O L O C B B P I Z R
Y J I K E M D P D P A G N Y M M O O V U
G O O V R E A J G O S W M H O S W E R S
S E L E C T R O M A G N E T I C E R I P
```

Waves	Sound	Reflected	Travel
Properties	Medium	Absorbed	Signals
Wavelength	Electromagnetic	Color	Pulses
Frequency	Radiation	Bends	Information
Amplitude	Light	Surface	Transmit

Spunky Science ™

ANSWER KEYS!

```
C E O J D E Y F L P T W E R U S S E R P
O S D I U Q I L J J A S R B O V I E P I T
N K I T C I C A U T C I M R E H T O X E
S W A T I R A F C O I N Y Q J G Q A J O P
E A G R O Y K W M K C Q E L S E D G P N
R P M S O O V H T C H E M I C A L L A I O
V M B E F A L I J A E O I B K V I G V T
E R C R E W D G E L M Z S P L U B E I
D K C R A J X H C R I S A J F T R E N I
P G R R E Z P W K P U R E C V A H S P O S
A A I S K H Y H D A T L K J X N S A H P O
A L P S E R U T C U R T S P O K M V E M
Z I A G K L N O K O O B V V V L O S W C
C D W P F B B M R E A C T I O N S A S
M S E I A T X S L A N O I T R O P O R P
```

Word bank (Matter & Its Interactions):

Atomic	Pure	Inert	Endothermic
Composition	Chemical	Pressure	Exothermic
Molecules	Liquids	Reactions	Crystals
Structures	Gases	Process	Transferred
Atoms		Conserved	Proportional

```
P M A G N E T I C L C D C L S T R E X E
A L S O A O K T R V F G K V Y O I F Q U
T N K A D I S T A N C E R H R O I S A L
T E L E C T R O M A G N E T I C N S U D
R H J M P C S V X C H A R G E S O T K E
A O U I O N W H D B T U I S O O G E Q S
C P I R Z G O N T C R S R T B H I E N A
T H O F H D P T R I E D E T R O C H L X
I Z B M O T I O N E O P N C E C N I I S
V S A D E O W D T I S S I V E N D B O A
E M N N E S N Q I O A H S I R E T Q T L
M N L K O S H V Z O P N N F A Y O A J R E
L K E L P S S D N N R S P E P D Y O Q E
N R A I I A N E B E A C S T C E J B O I
T D W V O H M L A N O I T A T I V A R G
```

Word bank (Motion & Stability):

Forces	Newton	Attractive	Distance
Motion	Law	Repulsive	Gravitational
Objects	Position	Magnitude	Electromagnetic
Equal	Electric	Charges	Strength
Exerts	Magnetic	Current	Masses

```
P I V E N V I R O N M E N T L T G O T A
A S A V S I S J H R O G O L P A M I U W
R A X E I W L F A O B J E C T S F S I E H
T W E F I T D E X Z T W R O C O F F C H J
I F B L U G T X E S V A R A T H D G J H F
C B J E L T I V R L D S E S Z E E V J F D
L Y U P R O P O R T I O N A L X G N D K F
E U L M R J L O G N I V O M C M U I Y Y
S L O M A V E R A G E B R N V B N Y N B
W L Y P K J F P V L R T M R G F E Y B F
X M D E E P O S Z Q D H R E U R R F G O
A Z L X F G K A S N Z W C I T E N E K R
A M A T T E R T A A A Q O A W F F D S C
S P K J A G B L Q M R W W S S S U O E E
F F L Q Q D V M T O I T E O T D P Y V G
C O L D E R Q T M M N O I T I S O P U F
```

Word bank (Energy):

Motion	Speed	Particles	Colder
Energy	Stored	Transfer	Forces
Proportional	Relative	Matter	Objects
Mass	Position	Environment	Moving
Average	Kinetic	Hotter	

```
P W A V E L E N G T H G O R O C R S U A
L H I I J E H T W X R F P E S M E W T W
E K O O L V K H A C J A S S O S G U O M
N L T A L C P F V O J V L E K D S N A E
D P M E K D R S Y L K I H L I L A N A D
S M I T P Z O S I J G S O U N D H E R I
I D I X T P N O T J T E O F T G I D U U
G W I A M U O R U O I V I A Y I R D Z M
N X F M D P T S T Y C N E U Q E R F A C
A F T H J C E A K W E B N I I C E S M Z
L Q I J K E M I L A R O L O C B B P I Z
O K T H J E M D P D P A G N Y M M O O V
K Y J I K R E A J G O S W M H O S W E R
G O O V R E A J G O S W M H O S W E R I
S E L E C T R O M A G N E T I C E R I P
```

Word bank (Waves):

Waves	Sound	Reflected	Travel
Properties	Medium	Absorbed	Signals
Wavelength	Electromagnetic	Color	Pulses
Frequency	Radiation	Bends	Information
Amplitude	Light	Surface	Transmit

Made in the USA
Las Vegas, NV
01 December 2024

13058277R00050